Prayers of the Faithful

Year A

Hugh McGinlay

Desbooks

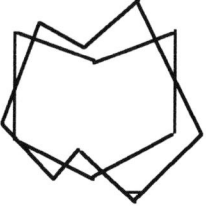

Published by
DESBOOKS
56 Wales Street
Thornbury 3071
Australia

ISBN: 0 949824 27 5

Prayers of the Faithful, Year A

First printed 1998.
Design and setting by Desbooks.
Printed by Gill Miller Press, Melbourne.

Contents

Prayers for other feast days may be found in *Prayers of the Faithful*, Years B and C.

Introduction

These prayers have been around in various formats for more than three years. First written for use in St Joseph's Parish in Northcote, Victoria, they were later offered to other parishes and schools where priests and other ministers and teachers have found them a useful addition or supplement to more traditional prayers.

The format of the prayers is simple. As a general rule, the four prayers pick up some of the themes of each of the four readings. The first prayer relates to the first reading; the second prayer to the second reading; the third and fourth prayer to the gospel reading of the day. Exceptions happen on major festivals of the church when the theme of the Sunday is reflected in each of the readings and prayers.

In writing the prayers, I have been concerned to highlight the Bible teaching in a way that makes it accessible in a prayer form as well as reminding the congregation of the reading they listened to earlier in the service. I have also had in mind that the prayer would use inclusive language as much as possible while remaining faithful to a tradition that has at its heart a belief in God revealed as Father, Son and Spirit.

The lay out of the prayer deliberately uses 'sense lines'. This encourages the reader to read the prayers in ways that makes their meaning easy to understand, suggesting a slight pause at the end of each line.

The prayer are not exhaustive for the Sunday. There is obviously room for other petitions - local or universal - and parishes and schools will have their own concerns to mention. They will also know that there is a variety of appropriate responses (sung as well as spoken) that can replace the formal 'Lord, hear us' that has been used here.

I gratefully acknowledge the many priests and lay people throughout Australia who have encouraged me in this ministry. I acknowledge in a special way the support of my wife Andrea and our sons Hugh and Danny.

Hugh McGinlay
Advent 1998

Year A

Advent 1

Priest/leader: 'The Son of man is coming
at an hour you do not expect!'
God's Word has been broken for us
and we are urged to prepare for the Lord's coming.
In a spirit of hope and fear,
we ask for what we need
to prepare for his coming.

1. For God's gift of peace.
(pause)

Nation will not lift sword against nation,
says the Lord.
May we be moved by the promises of God
to work for peace in our world.
and to long for that inner joy that comes
from doing what God wants.
Lord, hear us.

2. For the gift of being ready to welcome the Christ.
(pause)

Our salvation is near, says St Paul,
and we ask for the gift of being ready
to welcome Christ into our hearts
by a renewal of our desire
to live by the gospel.
Lord, hear us.

3. For the gift of hope.
(pause)

God promises life to those who walk in the light.
May we be people of the light,
eager to live as God wants,
confident of God's power to overcome all evil.
Lord, hear us.

4. For the gift of repentance.
(pause)

As we prepare for the coming of the Christ,
may we be conscious of what we value in life
and may we resolve in this time of Advent
to be faithful followers of the Lord
who is the light of the world.
Lord, hear us.

Priest/leader: God of the promises,
you teach us to hold on to what is true.
Grant what we need to be faithful
in following the Christ.
We ask this through Christ our Lord. Amen.

Advent 1

Advent 2

Priest/leader: 'Prepare a way for the Lord.'

God's Word has been broken for us
and its message calls for repentance.
In a spirit of renewal
we turn to the Lord
for our needs in the church and in the world.

1. For a sense of wonder at God's coming.
(pause)

May we examine ourselves carefully in this time of Advent
to discover what is of real importance in life;
and by lives of integrity and faithfulness
prepare a way for the Lord.
Lord, hear us.

2. For the gift of hope.
(pause)

May we be people of hope,
acknowledging God's power to fulfil the ancient promises
and may we so forgive and accept one another
that God may be glorified
and Jesus proclaimed in our lives.
Lord, hear us.

3. For a sense of repentance.
(pause)

John the Baptist proclaims a message
that demands obedience to the teaching of the Lord.
May we resolve in this time of Advent
to be guided by gospel values
and to live the way of Christ.
Lord, hear us.

4. For an understanding of what is important in life.
(pause)

As we prepare for Christmas
may we take to heart the preaching of the Baptist
examining ourselves in the light of his teaching
to uncover what is of lasting value in God's sight.
Lord, hear us.

Priest/leader: God of the promises,
you fill us with hope and expectancy at this time.
Help us appreciate what is important in life
and grant what we need.
Through Christ our Lord. Amen.

Advent 2

Year A

Advent 3

Priest /leader: 'Happy are those who do not lose faith in me.'

In this time of Advent,
God's Word brings comfort and challenge.
Nourished by its teaching
we turn to our God
for what we need.

1. For courage to follow the Lord.
(pause)

In this time of Advent,
may we be renewed in our resolve
to follow the Lord and listen to his teaching.
And may we be strengthened
by our faith in the God who saves us.
Lord, hear us.

2. For patience in this time of waiting.
(pause)

In this time of Advent,
may we be patience as we wait for the Lord,
knowing that our faith is not based on empty promises
but on the powerful Word of our God who saves.
Lord, hear us.

3. For a strengthening of our faith.
(pause)

In this time of Advent,
may we deepen our faith in Jesus, the Christ sent by God,
and recalling God's power at work in him,
may we resolve to listen to his teaching
and live as he commands.
Lord, hear us.

4. For a desire to prepare the way of the Lord.
(pause)

In this time of Advent,
may we be a people of the Way
determined to spread the good news of the Christ
by lives that reflect his integrity, his justice
and his commitment to do always what God commands.
Lord, hear us.

Priest/leader: Eternal God,
you are kind to us in every age.
In this time of Advent,
convince us about what is of lasting value
and grant what we need.
Through Christ our Lord. Amen.

Advent 3

Advent 4

Priest /leader:'His name is Emmanuel - God with us.'

The Word of God has been broken for us
and nourishes us with its Good News.
As we wait for the Lord's coming,
we turn to our God for our needs
in the church and in the world.

1. For an openness to what God wants of us.
(pause)

May we be alert to the signs of the times,
striving to discover what God wants
for the church and the world;
and eager to do what God commands.
Lord, hear us.

2. For a desire to preach the good news.
(pause)

Like Paul, we are called to preach the good news.
May our lives reflect the teaching of the gospel
by our integrity, our honesty
and our faithfulness to the example of Christ.
Lord, hear us.

3. For a sense of what is important at Christmas.
(pause)

As we approach the celebration of Christ's birth,
may we deepen our understanding of what is of value in life;
and may we be guided in our lives
not by what the world expects
but by what the gospel demands.
Lord, hear us.

4. For an appreciation of God with us.
(pause)

In these last days of Advent,
may we be filled with joy and peace
as we acknowledge the goodness of our God
who never abandons us,
especially in time of trouble.
Lord, hear us.

Priest/leader: God of all goodness,
you are with your people always.
Fill us with your peace at this time
and make us worthy to celebrate
the birth of your Son.
We ask this through Christ our Lord. Amen.

Advent 4

Year A

Christmas

Priest/leader:
'Today a Saviour has been born to us,
Christ the Lord.'
On this holy day,
we have listened with joy to God's good news.
With renewed confidence
we bring before our God
our needs and those of all the world.

1. For joy and peace at Christmas.
(pause)

May this be for us and for all people
a time of joy and peace
and may all the nations of the earth
rejoice at the birth of Christ.
Lord, hear us.

2. For a renewed sense of hope in our world.
(pause)

May our celebration of the birth of Jesus
be an occasion for renewed hope in our world;
and may our joy and our witness
bring the good news of salvation
to the whole human race.
Lord, hear us.

3. For those in sorrow at this time.
(pause)

We recall those who are in sorrow or trouble
at this time -
those who are mourning the loss of family and friends;
those who are homeless and unemployed;
those who are sick.
Lord, hear us.

4. For peace in our families.
(Pause)

May we experience peace in our families
at this special time,
and may the spirit of Christmas
be with our families and communities
throughout the year ahead.
Lord, hear us.

Priest/leader: Mighty God and prince of peace,
our hearts are filled with joy and confidence
as we make our prayers to you on this special day,
for you are Lord for ever and ever. Amen.

Christmas

1 January Mary, Mother of God.

Year A

Priest/leader: On this festival of Mary, Mother of God,
we have listened to God's Word
and been nourished by its teaching.
With Mary as our example
we turn to the Lord in prayer.

1. For a true devotion to Mary, Mother of God.
(pause)

Mary is the instrument of God's blessing.
May we learn from her example
by trying to discover what God wants of us
and by lives of gentleness, prayer and service.
Lord, hear us.

2. For the gift of being thankful.
(pause)

May we be aware of the blessings of God in our lives
and with Mary as our mother
thank God for the gift of the Son
to be our Saviour and our brother.
Lord, hear us.

3. For those who care for children in our community.
(pause)

May we always be thankful to God
for those who care for children in our community.
With Mary our mother to guide them
may they be strong in their love
and constant in their care.
Lord, hear us.

4. For an openness towards God.
(pause)

Mary said yes to God
when the angel asked her to be mother of the Messiah.
May we be open to God's promptings in life
and learn to accept God's purposes
especially in time of trouble.
Lord, hear us.

Priest/leader: God of all consolation,
we honour Mary, mother of the saviour and our mother.
Listen to our prayers for we make them
in the name of her Son, Jesus Christ our Lord. Amen.

Mary,
Mother of
God

Year A

Christmas 1 (The Holy Family)

Priest/leader:
'Let the message of Christ, in all its fullness, find a home in you.'

In this season of Christmas,
we thank our God for the gift of Jesus.
Today we open ourselves to God's Word
telling us how we are to live
as children of God in families of love.

1. For respect and acceptance in families.
(pause)

We pray for all members of our families.
May parents and children respect and honour one another
for their lives and their gifts.
May we care for our parents in time of need
and love them as the Lord loves us.
Lord, hear us.

2. For forgiveness and love in family life.
(pause)

All families are blessed by God
for forgiveness, patience and gentleness.
May we be gentle in our families
- especially at this time of Christmas -
accepting one another as the Lord accepts us.
Lord, hear us.

3. For the grace to be witnesses in life.
(pause)

May our families live by the teaching of the gospel
witnessing to one another
in prayer, acceptance and forgiveness.
May we teach one another
how we are to live as children of God
and brothers and sisters of Christ.
Lord, hear us.

4. For families in need.
(pause)

As God's people in this place,
may we support families in need.
May we be generous with our time and resources
when families are bereaved or in distress.
Lord, hear us.

Priest/leader:
God of the promises,
we bring the needs of all families before you,
with all their shapes and differences.
Bless our families and help us be faithful
to the teaching of your Son.
We ask this through Christ our Lord. Amen.

Christmas 1

Christmas 2

Priest /leader: 'John came as a witness
a witness to the light.'

God's Word has been made flesh for us
in Jesus of Nazareth.
Filled with hope at the fulfilment of the ancient promises
we turn to our God with confidence
for what we need.

1. For the gift of wisdom.
(pause)

The gift of wisdom
is given to God's's people in every age.
May we learn to read the signs of the time
and to discern God's will
for the church and for the world.
Lord, hear us.

2. For an awareness that we are God's children.
(pause)

God has chosen us in Christ -
the adopted children of a loving Father.
May God grant us wisdom and understanding
and the knowledge we need
to witness to the gospel in our time.
Lord, hear us.

3. For a desire to live in the light.
(pause)

Christmas is a season of lights.
May we live as children of the light
witnessing to gospel teaching
by how we live
and what we value.
Lord, hear us.

4. For the gift of thanksgiving.
(pause)

In this Christmas season
may we renew our thanks to our God
for the gift of the Saviour
who teaches us how to live
and offers life in all its fulness.
Lord, hear us.

Priest/leader: God of our ancestors,
your Son is the light of the world.
May we live always according to his way.
Grant what we need.
Through Christ our Lord. Amen.

Christmas 2

Year A

Epiphany of the Lord

Priest/leader: 'The sight of the star filled them with delight.'
The good news of Jesus' birth
fills us with delight
and we have listened to God's Word broken for us.
Now we approach the Lord of the Universe
for our needs and those of all the world.

1. For peace in our world.
(pause)

May all the nations of the world
receive the light that God sends
and strive for peace in our time -
peace that only God can bring.
Lord, hear us.

2. For a renewed desire to serve in our world.
(pause)

May we who follow the infant King of the Jews
share his life of service
and by our witness to gospel values
bring all people to acknowledge his truth.
Lord, hear us.

3. For the Jewish people.
(pause)

May the people of Israel be faithful
to their ancient covenant with God
and may we who share God's blessing with them
always respect those
who were first to receive God's good news.
Lord, hear us.

4. For a sense of delight in God's presence.
(pause)

May we who celebrate this day
experience joy and delight in the presence of our king
and by the honesty and integrity of our lives
be faithful disciples of the Lord we worship.
Lord, hear us.

Priest/leader: God of the universe.
your good news is for all the peoples of the earth.
Hear our prayers this day and grant what we need.
Through Christ our Lord. Amen.

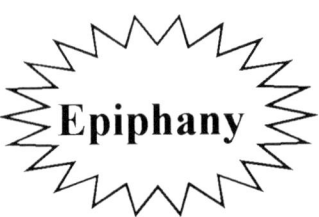
Epiphany

The Baptism of Jesus

Priest/leader: 'You are my Son, the beloved;
my favour rests on you.'

God's Word has been broken for us
on this celebration of the Lord's Baptism.
Its teaching strengthens our hope in our God
as we recall our needs for the church and the community.

1. For a desire to serve.
(pause)

Baptism is a call to serve.
May we be good servants of the Lord
who struggle for justice and peace in society
and look for ways to be of service
in the church and in the community.
Lord, hear us.

2. For tolerance in society.
(pause)

Baptism is a call to love.
May the teaching of the Scripture
that God has no favourites
remind us of the command to love one another
as God first loved us.
Lord, hear us.

3. For a desire to take the gospel seriously.
(pause)

Baptism is a call to new life.
May the Baptism of Jesus recall our own Baptism
when we chose to become followers of the Way
and to reflect gospel values
in all of our lives.
Lord, hear us.

4. For an openness to what God wants.
(pause)

Baptism is a call to faith.
Jesus struggled to understand
the implications of God's call.
May we too be open to what God wants
and, with God's help,
respond with generosity to that call.
Lord, hear us.

Priest/leader:
God of the promises,
we rejoice in the Baptism of your Son.
Make us eager to follow his way
and grant what we need.
Through Christ our Lord. Amen.

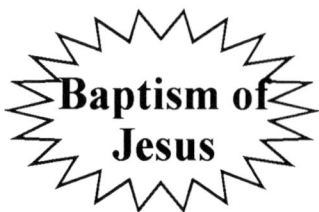

Ash Wednesday

Priest/leader: 'Turn from your sins
and believe the good news!'
This is God's Word to us today.
We have listened to that Word
and we turn to God in prayer.

1. For the grace to follow Christ
   in this journey through Lent.
(pause)

As we begin our forty days of Lent,
we ask God to raise in our minds
an awareness of sin in our lives
and the greatness of God's tender love.
Lord, hear us,

2. For the grace to take the journey seriously.
(pause)

We beg God's blessing on our journey
to help us take stock of our lives:
 - what is important for us
 - what controls us
 - what we need to do
to be faithful to the gospel
and followers of Christ.
Lord, hear us.

3. For the grace to grow in prayer.
(pause)

We ask the Lord to give us a spirit of prayer
that we might relish the time we spend in prayer,
not regarding it as a burden
but a time of joy and reflection
in the presence of the God who loves us.
Lord, hear us.

4. For a true spirit of penance during Lent.
(pause)

May we learn to follow the teaching of Jesus
and discipline ourselves during this time of Lent
by prayer and fasting and acts of charity
so that we might have a true understanding
of what is of lasting value in life
according to the mind of our Saviour.
Lord, hear us.

Priest/leader: Creator God,
our bodies have been marked today
with the ashes of repentance.
Listen to the prayers we have made
and in your love, help us in what we need.
Through Christ our Lord.
Amen.

Lent 1

Year A

Priest/ leader:
'You must worship the Lord and serve God alone!'
In this time of Lent,
God's Word insists on repentance
and change of heart.
Encouraged by its teaching,
we ask God for what we need.

1. For a desire not to be ruled by evil.
(pause)

By Adam's sin, evil entered our world
and threatens to dominate the earth.
By God's grace, may we not be ruled by sin
but resist its temptation to control our lives.
Lord, hear us.

2. For a deeper appreciation of what Christ has done for us.
(pause)

May we deepen our understanding
of what God has achieved in Christ
and by a renewed desire to follow his way,
overcome evil in the world
by lives of justice, integrity and truth.
Lord, hear us.

3. For a desire to grow in the love of God.
(pause)

In this time of Lent, may we grow closer to our God,
and by time spent in prayer and fasting
imitate our Master,
who found time to be alone
with the God who gives meaning to life.
Lord, hear us.

4. For an understanding of what is important in life.
(pause)

Jesus was tempted in the desert
to disobey the way of God.
By our obedience to the teaching of Christ,
may we deepen our appreciation and understanding
of what is of ultimate value in life.
Lord, hear us.

Priest/ leader: God of all consolation,
you comforted your Son
in his temptation.
Strengthen us in our resolve
to follow him faithfully.
We ask this through Christ our Lord. Amen.

Lent 1

Lent 2

Priest/leader:
'This is my Son, the Beloved. Listen to him.'
We have heard God's Word
and been nourished by its teaching.
We now reflect on what we need in our faith journey
and present our needs to our God.

1. For faith to live as God wants.
(pause)

Abraham left his country and all that was familiar
to go to the land promised by God.
May we grow in faith each day
trusting in God's goodness
and God's purposes for our lives.
Lord, hear us.

2. For faith in time of doubt.
(pause)

Paul commands us to rely on God's power
in time of trouble.
May the transfiguration renew our faith in God's promises
and give us courage to believe the Good News
at all times.
Lord, hear us.

3. For faith in Jesus, Son of God.
(pause)

Jesus is God's Son, the Beloved.
May we be open to his Word in this time of Lent,
listening for his teaching
and eager to renew our confidence
in the one who enjoys God's favour.
Lord, hear us.

4. For faith in God's kindness.
(pause)

Jesus commands us: 'Do not be afraid'.
May we grow in understanding God's goodness and kindness;
and may we overcome fear in our lives
recalling the resurrection of God's Son
and his triumph over evil and death.
Lord, hear us.

Priest/leader:
God of our ancestors,
you are faithful in every age.
Grant what we need to be your faithful people.
Through Christ our Lord. Amen.

Lent 2

Lent 3

Priest/leader:
'My food is to do the will of the one who sent me.'

The words of Jesus comfort us and challenge us.
Nourished by the teaching we have heard,
we turn to our God for what we need.

1. For a deepening of our faith in God.
(pause)

God cared for the people of Israel,
providing water for them in their time of need.
May we grow in faith in our God who loves us
and who provides for us in all of life.
Lord, hear us.

2. For a desire to be at peace with God.
(pause)

Through the work of Christ, we are at peace with God.
May this sense of peace fill us with confidence during Lent
and may we remember the lengths to which God has gone
to show love for us.
Lord, hear us.

3. For a sense of urgency in living the gospel.
(pause)

Jesus reached out to the Samaritan woman
and longed for her to acknowledge
the truth about God.
By our lives of faithfulness to his teaching
may people everywhere come to accept Jesus
as the Christ of God.
Lord, hear us.

4. For an acceptance of all people.
(pause)

By talking with the Samaritan woman,
Jesus overcame barriers of hatred and exclusion.
May we be accepting of all people,
faithful to Jesus' command
to love one another as God loves us.
Lord, hear us.

Priest/leader: God of all nations,
may your kingdom come!
Teach us to be tolerant,
open and faithful to your way.
Grant what we need.
Through Christ our Lord. Amen.

Lent 3

Year A

Lent 4

Priest/leader:
'The Lord is my shepherd; there is nothing I shall want.'
Encouraged by this teaching
and strengthened by God's Word.
we reflect on what we need
in the church and in the community.

1. For the gift to understand God's ways.
(pause)

God's ways are not our ways
and God's choices are not what we expect.
May we be alert to the God of surprises
and open to God's purposes
for the church and for the world.
Lord, hear us.

2. For the gift to live as children of the light.
(pause)

God commands us to live by the light of the gospel,
overcoming darkness and sin in our lives.
In this time of Lent,
may we resolve to walk in the light of Christ
and to proclaim the light
by our faithfulness to Christ's teaching.
Lord, hear us.

3. For the gift to see what God wants.
(pause)

Jesus is the light of the world
and his teaching is our best guide in life.
May we grow in understanding his way
eager to live as God wants
and to choose what is right
according to God's law.
Lord, hear us.

4. For the gift of perseverance.
(pause)

The man born blind was rejected by his companions
because he professed faith in Jesus.
May we persevere in faith
and in living the gospel
especially when the teaching is not popular
and rejected in society.
Lord, hear us.

Priest/leader: God of mercy,
take pity upon us
and strengthen our faith.
Grant what we neeed.
Through Christ our Lord. Amen.

Lent 4

Lent 5

Priest/leader:
'Anyone who believes in me
will never die.'
This teaching of the Lord
encourages us and strengthens us in life.
Nourished by God's Word,
we ask our God for what we need.

1. For an openness to God's Spirit.
(pause)

It is God's Spirit that gives life.
May we be open to God at work in our lives
and by overcoming sin and death
in what we do and what we choose
may God be glorified and God's purposes fulfilled.
Lord, hear us.

2. For a desire to be possessed by God's Spirit.
(pause)

May we be faithful to God's way
and to the teaching of the gospel
that God's Spirit may possess us entirely
enabling us to be faithful witnesses
of our God who loves us.
Lord, hear us.

3. For faith in Jesus, the giver of life.
(pause)

Jesus raised Lazarus to life
breaking the bonds of death
and setting him free.
By our faith in Jesus,
and our faithfulness to his teaching
may we be free from sin and selfishness,
living as God wants in the church and in the community.
Lord, hear us.

4. For a desire to witness to the Lord.
(pause)

Martha and Mary confessed their faith in Jesus.
Like them, may we acknowledge him
as the Lord of life
and with confidence in his love
commend ourselves and those we love
to his care.
Lord, hear us.

Priest/leader: God of compassion,
you care for all your children.
Fill us with confidence in your power to save us
and grant what we need,
Through Christ our Lord. Amen.

Lent 5

Year A

Lent 6 (Passion/Palm Sunday)

Priest/leader:
We have begun our Holy Week observances.
We have celebrated Jesus' entry to Jerusalem
and watched the mood change from joy to sadness.
Yet in a spirit of hope, we present our needs before our God.

1. For Christian people everywhere.
(pause)

At the beginning of this Holy Week,
we pray for all our Christian brothers and sisters
that we may follow the example of Jesus
who emptied himself for us
that we may learn to be one with each other
in the service of all.
Lord, hear us.

2. For those who suffer for what they believe.
(pause)

We pray for those in our world
who, like Jesus, are unjustly persecuted
for what they hold dearest.
By our prayers and actions,
may we be in solidarity with them
who suffer for justice and truth.
Lord, hear us.

3. For a sense of peace in the midst of suffering.
(pause)

May we be granted the gift of inner peace
when we experience pain at the hands of others.
And may Christians everywhere
support those who are suffering
by our patience and understanding and love.
Lord, hear us.

4. For a fruitful observance of Holy Week
(pause)

May we use this Holy Week profitably
- for reflection and prayer
- for renewal and repentance
- for acts of charity
- for worship and sharing.
Lord, hear us.

Priest/leader: God of compassion,
keep us faithful even in times of suffering
and bring us to Easter joy.
We ask this through Christ our Lord. Amen.

Lent 6

Holy Thursday

Priest/leader: On this holy night
we remember with joy the Supper of the Lord.
Gathered as God's people
and refreshed by the breaking of God's Word
we recall our needs
and the needs of the church.

1. For a spirit of service.
(pause)

Jesus the Master washed the feet
of his disciples.
May we learn from him that God's ways
demands service to others
in the community and in the church.
Lord, hear us.

2. For those called to ministry in the churches.
(pause)

May all who are ordained to ministry in the churches
be wise leaders in the community,
people of integrity and faith
eager to share God's Word
with their fellow servants
in the church.
Lord, hear us.

3. For a renewal in our following of Christ.
(pause)

Jesus gave us a new commandment
to love one another has he loved us.
May we deepen our desire to live that commandment
that people everywhere may recognise us
as followers of Christ.
Lord, hear us.

4. For a desire to be broken for others.
(pause)

May the broken bread and the outpoured wine
be symbols of God's people
willing to be broken and poured out
for the service of the world.
Lord, hear us.

Priest/leader: Ruler of the Universe, God most high,
we thank you for your love
for all the world.
Give us the strength we need
to be your faithful witnesses.
We ask this through Christ our Lord. Amen.

Year A

General Intercessions for Good Friday

1. For the church
Let us pray for God's church all over the world.
(pause)

Lord, guide your church throughout the world.
May the church proclaim your good news
and bring your salvation to all people.
We ask this through Christ our Lord. Amen.

2. For the leaders in the churches,
Let us pray for the leaders in the Christian churches:
for the Pope, the patriarchs of the Orthodox Churches,
the Archbishop of Canterbury, and
the leaders of the Protestant Churches.
(pause)

Lord, Guide the Pope
and all the leaders in the churches.
May their preaching and their example
help us grow in faith
and become more faithful followers of your Son.
We ask this through Christ our Lord. Amen.

3. For all members of the churches.
Let us pray for all who belong
to the people of God.
(pause)

Lord, your Spirit guides the church
and makes it holy.
Help us to be faithful witnesses
to the way of Jesus
in what we do and what we value.
We ask this through Christ our Lord. Amen.

4. For those preparing for Baptism.
Let us pray for those people
who are preparing for Baptism.
(pause)

Lord, you constantly bless your church
with new members.
Increase the faith and understanding of those
preparing for Baptism at this time.
We ask this through Christ our Lord. Amen.

5. For unity among Christians.
(pause)

Look with favour on all
who follow the way of your Son
and share the same Baptism
Bring us all to the fullness of faith
and keep us one in the bonds of love.
We ask this through Christ our Lord. Amen.

Good
Friday

6. For the Jewish people.
Let us pray for the Jewish people
the first to hear God's Word
and share the covenant.
(pause)

Lord, long ago you gave the promises
to Abraham and to his descendants for ever.
We pray for our Jewish brothers and sisters
as they strive to be faithful to your covenant with them,
We ask this through Christ our Lord. Amen.

7. For those who not believe in Christ.
Let us pray for those
who do not believe in Christ
that they may be shown the way to salvation.
(pause)

We pray for our brothers and sisters
who do not acknowledge Christ in their hearts.
By our witness to his teaching
may they discover the truth about Jesus
and walk in his ways.
We ask this through Christ our Lord. Amen.

8. For those who do not believe in God.
Let us pray for those who do not believe in God
that they may find God by following
what is right in their hearts.
(pause)

Lord, you created people to know you
and to enjoy peace in your love.
May our faithfulness in reflecting your love and mercy
bring those who do not believe in you
to acknowledge you as Lord and God of all.
We ask this through Christ our Lord. Amen.

9. For those in public office
Let us pray for those who serve the community in public office.
(pause)

Lord, in your goodness,
watch over those in public office
so that people everywhere
may know freedom, security and peace.
We ask this through Christ our Lord. Amen.

10. For those in special need.
Let us pray for the sick, the dying,
those who suffer in war and famine
and all who need our prayers at this time.
(pause)

Lord, give strength to the weary
and new courage to those who have lost heart.
We commend to you all who are in need
in our world and in our community.
We ask this through Christ our Lord. Amen.

Year A

Easter Vigil

Priest/leader:
The Lord is risen! heaven and earth rejoice
in the reconciliation of God
with all creation.
Filled with Easter joy
we bring to God our needs
for the church and for the world.

1. For the community that is called the church.
(pause)

We are an Easter people
and we ask God's blessing in the church.
May it be a source of joy and hope
in a world of despair.
Lord, hear us.

2. For new Christians
(pause)

May those who have been baptised this night
know the peace that only God can give
and may they be faithful
to the promises they have made.
Lord, hear us.

3. For a deeper faith in the risen Christ.
(pause)

By the death of Jesus, sin has been destroyed
and has power over us no longer.
Strengthened by faith
may we live no longer as slaves of sin
but alive for God in Christ Jesus.
Lord, hear us.

4. For the world in darkness.
(pause)

May the light of Christ so shine
in our lives and in the church
that people everywhere will be comforted
by our charity and our kindness.
Lord, hear us.

Priest/leader: Creator God of heaven and earth,
we bless you and thank you for this holy night.
Be with us always and help us be faithful witnesses
to the risen Christ.
We ask this through Christ our Lord. Amen.

Easter
Vigil

Easter Day

Priest/leader: Christ our hope is risen! Alleluia!
In our rejoicing at the resurrection of our Saviour,
we turn to God and recall our needs
and those of all the church.

1. For the church throughout the world.
(pause)

On this Easter Day,
may Christians everywhere experience
the joy of the risen Christ
and be renewed in faith and hope.
Lord, hear us.

2. For those in trouble at this time.
(pause)

May the triumph of Christ over death
be a comfort to those who are in distress
or are suffering at this time.
Lord, hear us.

3. For a desire to live a new life in Christ.
(pause)

May this Easter Day
inspire us to grow in Christ
so that like him
we may choose to walk in the light
and avoid the darkness of sin.
Lord, hear us.

4. For a commitment to be witnesses to Christ.
(pause)

May we share the enthusiasm of Mary Magdalene
to be witnesses to the resurrection of Jesus
by our faithfulness to his teaching
and our living of gospel values.
Lord, hear us.

Priest/leader: God of all hope,
you raised Jesus to newness of life.
Send your Spirit into our hearts
that even in troubled times,
we may be people of hope.
Through Christ our Lord. Amen.

Year A

Easter 2

Priest/leader: 'My Lord and my God.'
With Thomas, we confess Jesus
as Lord and Christ.
Strengthened by the message of God's Word,
broken for us,
we turn to our God
for what we need.

1. For the gift of generosity.
(pause)

The first Christians were generous towards one another,
sharing what they owned for the love of God.
May we too be people of kindness
known for our concern for the poor and the helpless
and generous in sharing what we have.
Lord, hear us.

2. For the gift of hope and joy.
(pause)

The resurrection of Jesus fills us with hope and joy.
May the good news of Jesus raised from the dead
console us in time of trial
and remind us of God's great love
especially in time of sorrow and loss.
Lord, hear us.

3. For the gift of faith.
(pause)

Like Thomas, we long to see the risen Christ.
May we grow in faith,
recognising him in the broken bread
and the wine shared -
an everlasting sign of God's presence with the people.
Lord, hear us.

4. For the gift of forgiveness.
(pause)

Jesus commanded his followers to forgive one another.
May we be a people of forgiveness,
accepting one another in love
not bearing grudges
but striving to live in peace with all peoples.
Lord, hear us.

Priest/leader: God of life and love,
your Spirit fills us with confidence.
Listen to the prayers we make
and grant what we need.
Through Christ our Lord. Amen.

Easter 2

Easter 3

Priest/leader:
'They recognised Jesus at the breaking of the bread.'
As God's people, we gather
to break the bread that is the Christ of God.
Nourished by God's Word broken for us
we commend ourselves to our Lord.

1. For a deeper understanding of Jesus' resurrection.
(pause)

In this Easter season, may we grow in faith and understanding
about Christ risen from the dead.
May we acknowledge God's purposes at work in him -
in his life, his teaching, his death and resurrection -
and may we be faithful in our following of his way.
Lord, hear us.

2. For a deeper understanding of the price of our salvation.
(pause)

God sent his son Jesus
to free us from sin and death.
Acknowledging that it cost the death of the sinless one,
may we be constant in praising God
for what has been done for us in Christ.
Lord, hear us.

3. For a deeper understanding about Christ crucified.
(pause)

May we seek to understand the purposes of God
who allowed Christ to be crucified and to die for us.
May we be comforted by the depths of God's love for us
and strengthened by the good news of the resurrection.
Lord, hear us.

4. For a deeper understanding of Christ present among us.
(pause)

May we grow in faith about Christ present among us
and like the apostles on the road to Emmaus
be strengthened in life's journey
by the knowledge that Christ is with us
especially in the breaking of the bread.
Lord, hear us.

Priest/leader: God of the promises,
you are with us always.
Strengthen our faith in your love
and grant what we need.
Through Christ our Lord. Amen.

Easter 3

Easter 4

Priest/leader:
'I have come so that you may have life in its fullness.'
The good news of Jesus the shepherd
encourages us in our journey through life.
Strengthened by the teaching of the Bible,
we are confident before our God,
asking for what we need.

1. For a desire to renew our Baptismal promises.
(pause)

Peter proclaimed Jesus as Lord and Christ.
By our Baptism, we have put on Christ
and refused to be dominated by sin.
In this Easter time, we renew that commitment,
asking God's grace to be faithful to our Baptism.
Lord, hear us.

2. For a desire to understand the sufferings of Jesus.
(pause)

The sufferings of Jesus
are part of the mysterious purposes of God.
May we strive to imitate him
when suffering and sorrow are part of our lives,
and, like our Master, may we put our trust
in the merciful love of God.
Lord, hear us.

3. For a desire to follow Christ the shepherd.
(pause)

May we acknowledge Christ as our shepherd,
the one who is the way to life,
and by our faithfulness to his teaching,
may others be attracted to accept him
as the Christ of God.
Lord, hear us.

4. For a desire to witness to the truth.
(pause)

Christ is the holy one of God,
the teacher and shepherd of all.
By lives that reflect gospel values
may we bear witness to the truth that he spoke
and the fullness of life that he promised.
Lord, hear us.

Priest/leader: God of compassion,
look on us with favour
as we try to imitate your son;
and grant what we need.
Through Christ our Lord. Amen.

Easter 4

Easter 5

Priest/leader: 'I am the way, the truth and the life.'

God's holy Word has been broken for us
and we are nourished by its teaching.
Filled with Easter joy, we turn to our God
for what we need in the church and community.

1. For a spirit of service to others.
(pause)

The first Christians shared all they possessed
and were committed to being of service to one another.
May service be the mark of all our Christian lives
not only in the church but in the wider society.
Lord, hear us.

2. For a spirit of openness to God.
(pause)

Jesus is the stone rejected by others
yet chosen by God to be the key stone in the kingdom.
May we be open to God's choices
for the church and for the world,
eager to walk in the light of the gospel
according to God's call.
Lord, hear us.

3. For a spirit of trust in God's promises.
(pause)

Jesus commands us not to be troubled.
May our confidence in God be strengthened
and our hope confirmed
in the promise God has made
for those who follow the way of Christ.
Lord, hear us.

4. For a spirit of truth in our lives.
(pause)
Jesus is the way, the truth and the life.
May we be a people dedicated to the truth
about God, about the Christ
and about God's purposes
for all the people in the world.
Lord, hear us.

Priest/leader:
God of the promises,
you have loved all your creation from the beginning.
Renew our hope in you
and grant what we need.
Through Christ our Lord. Amen.

Easter 5

Year A

Easter 6

Priest/leader:
'I will not leave you orphans', says the Lord.
This good news comforts us especially in time of distress.
Strengthened by the teaching of the Word,
we turn with confidence to our God
for what we need.

1. For a desire to witness to the gospel.
(pause)

By lives that reflect gospel teaching
and the values of the way of Christ
may others be attracted to believing God's Word.
May they accept Baptism and the gift of God's Spirit
that brings happiness and true life in all its fullness.
Lord, hear us.

2. For a desire to reverence the Lord.
(pause)

Jesus was put to death for us
and rose to bring us new life.
May we always reverence the Lord Jesus in our hearts;
and by prayer and reflection
be confident in bearing witness to what we believe
about the Christ and the teaching we have received.
Lord, hear us.

3. For a desire to keep the commandments.
(pause)

May we strive always to obey the commandments of the Lord,
especially the commandments about love and service;
and in this way show forth our love for the Christ
and our faith in his teaching that brings life forever.
Lord, hear us.

4. For a desire to prepare for the coming of the Spirit.
(pause)

Jesus promised to send another Advocate,
the Spirit of truth who would be with us in the community.
By our witness to the truth of the gospel,
and our faithfulness to the teaching of the Christ,
may we prepare well to celebrate the coming of God's Spirit.
Lord, hear us.

Priest/leader: God of love,
you have never left us
and your Spirit guides us always.
Listen to the prayers we make.
Through Christ our Lord. Amen.

Easter 6

The feast of the Ascension

Priest/leader:
'God has put all things under Christ's feet
and made him ruler of everything,
head of the church.'
As followers of Christ
we bring our prayers to our God.

1. For a deep sense of hope.
(pause)

We renew our faith in the God of the promises
and we ask for a deepening of the gift of hope.
May we be consoled by the knowledge of God's faithfulness.
and assured of sharing the glory
that is Christ's.
Lord, hear us.

2. For a greater awareness of God's love for all.
(pause)

Christ has been taken up to heaven
to be with God for ever.
May we who are his followers on earth
grow in understanding the mystery
of God's purpose for the world and for us
Lord, hear us.

3. For a desire to be witnesses to the gospel.
(pause)

We are commanded to go out to the world
proclaiming the good news of the Christ.
May we be faithful witnesses to him
and to all that the gospel requires.
Lord, hear us.

4. For a sense of joy in proclaiming the gospel.
(pause)

The apostles went back to Jerusalem full of joy.
May we too be people of joy
happy to live out the gospel message
by lives of faithfulness to God's Word.
Lord, hear us.

Priest/leader:
God of the promises
we worship you as our ruler and our head.
Be our consolation as we await
the coming of the Lord.
We ask this through Christ our Lord. Amen.

Ascension

Easter 7

Priest/leader: 'I am praying for them...
because they belong to you.'
The promises of God
comfort and strengthen us in life.
God's Word has been broken for us
and we are nourished by its teaching.
We turn to our God with confidence
for what we need.

1. For a spirit of prayer.
(pause)

The first Christians were devoted to prayer,
acknowledging it as central in the life of faith.
May we too relish the time spent in prayer,
recalling God's goodness to us
and discerning God's purposes for our lives.
Lord, hear us.

2. For a spirit of acceptance.
(pause)

Jesus suffered and died
for the truth about God.
May we be strengthened by his example
when we stand up for what we believe
and witness to the truth about the gospel.
Lord, hear us.

3. For a spirit of perseverance in life.
(pause)

Eternal life is to know God
and the Christ whom God has sent.
May we be strong in faith
and persevere in witnessing to the truth
so that God may be glorified
in the church and in the community.
Lord, hear us.

4. For a spirit of love for one another.
(pause)

May we be so filled with love for one another
that God's name may be held holy;
and may we hold on with firmness
to the teaching we have received
so that the work of Christ
may be continued in our time.
Lord, hear us.

Easter 7

Priest/leader: God of the promises,
your Son Jesus is the way to eternal life.
We glorify him and we glorify you.
Listen to our prayers
and grant what we need.
Through Christ our Lord. Amen.

Pentecost Day

Priest/leader:
Fifty days have passed since Easter.
We welcome God's Spirit among us
comforting, inspiring, consoling
and helping us as we pray to God
for what we need.

1. For an openness to God's Holy Spirit.
(pause)

The Spirit brings new life to the church
and renews the whole world.
May we be open to the promptings of the Spirit
and accept that the church is led by God's Spirit
towards the future known only to God.
Lord, hear us.

2. For a desire to make Christ known throughout the world.
(pause)

The people of Jerusalem heard the good news
in their own languages.
May we be constant in searching for ways
to make God known by language and preaching
that makes sense to people of today.
Lord, hear us.

3. For a spirit of forgiveness.
(pause)

The gift of the Holy Spirit is a gift of reconciliation.
May we reach out to our brothers and sisters
with forgiveness and tolerance
and be peace makers in our families,
our communities and our world.
Lord, hear us.

4. For a sense of renewal.
(pause)

The Spirit is God's gift for the renewal of the world.
May we grow in prayer; increase in faith;
and be ready to work
for what is good and just and holy
in the church and in our world.
Lord, hear us.

Priest/leader:
Come, Holy Spirit,
fill us with your loving presence.
Make us strong and constant followers of Christ,
on fire, like the apostles,
with desire to proclaim the gospel and to live it out.
We ask this through Christ our Lord. Amen.

Pentecost

Trinity Sunday

Priest/leader:
Everyone who is moved by God's Spirit
is not God's slave but God's child.
As children of God we approach our God
with confidence and without fear,
asking for those things we need
as God's people in God's world.

1. For a respect for the name of God.
(pause)

We worship God - three yet one -
and we praise the name of God.
May our love for God
and our concern for God's creation
shine out in our world.
Lord, hear us.

2. For trust in the faithfulness of God
(pause)

May we live in reverence of the Lord,
our help and our shield,
and place all our hope in God.
Lord, hear us

3. For a childlike spirit in our attitude to God.
(pause)

We are God's children, chosen in Christ our brother.
May we reverence our God with wonder
but be filled with confidence and trust.
Lord, hear us.

4. For a sense of God's presence.
(pause)

As we live in response to God's commands
may we be more and more aware
that the Lord is with us to the end of time.
Lord, hear us.

Priest/leader:
Creator God, may your name be held holy!
May your kingdom come!
Listen to the prayers we make this day
through Christ our Lord. Amen.

Trinity
Sunday

Body and Blood of Christ

Priest/leader:
Jesus is our high priest,
whose precious blood
has established for us
an everlasting covenant with God.
As people of the covenant,
we bring our prayers before the Lord.

1. For a deeper awareness of God's covenant of love.
(pause)

The people of Israel sealed the covenant with God
using the blood of chosen animals.
May we learn from the shedding of Christ's blood
how great is the love of God
for all the people of the world.
Lord, hear us.

2. For a greater understanding of the sacrifice of Christ.
(pause)

The blood of Christ makes us holy before God.
May we grow in our understanding
of what Christ achieved for us
by his life and death.
May our sharing in the sacrament
increase our service to God and one another.
Lord, hear us.

3. For a love of the Eucharist.
(pause)

Jesus commanded us to share his body and blood
in memory of him.
May we learn to love this central act of worship
and to live out its command of love
in all that we do.
Lord, hear us.

4. For a desire to be more faithful to the covenant.
(pause)

We are nourished by the body and blood of the Lord.
May our sharing in this sacrament
make us active in living out
the Lord's command to love one another.
Lord, hear us.

Priest/leader:
God of the covenant,
you give us this sacrament as a sign of your love for us.
May we grow in love, eager to worship you
by our care for one another.
We ask this through Christ our Lord Amen.

Corpus Christi

Sunday 2

Priest/leader: 'Jesus is the chosen one of God.'

The Word of God gives us life and joy.
We have listened to its teaching
and professed our faith
in the God who makes us whole.
With confidence, we turn to our God
for what we need.

1. For a desire to witness to the gospel.
(pause)

We are the people of God,
called to be a light to the nations.
By our faithfulness to the teaching of the gospel
may God be glorified
and all people acknowledge God's Son
as Lord of life.
Lord, hear us.

2. For a desire to be of service.
(pause)

God calls us to be servants of one another
in the community of saints that is the church.
May our love and acceptance of one another
make us worthy to be the people of God.
Lord, hear us.

3. For a desire to be followers of Christ.
(pause)

Jesus is the lamb of God
who takes away the sin of the world.
May we be faithful followers of the lamb
refusing to be controlled by sin and evil
but eager, like him, to be a light for the world.
Lord, hear us.

4. For a desire to make Christ known in the world.
(pause)

Jesus is the chosen one of God,
the model of faithful service
in the church and in the world.
May we so follow his teaching and example
that people everywhere will come to know
the truth about God and about the Christ.
Lord, hear us.

Priest/leader: God of the promises,
help us in our desire
to be faithful followers of your Son
who lives and reigns
for ever and ever. Amen.

Sunday 3

Priest/leader: 'I will make you fishers of all people.'

God's Word challenges us to take seriously
the way of Christ.
Nourished by its teaching
we look to our God
for what we need.

1. For a sense of joy in following the Lord.
(pause)

Christ is our light
and we are the people who walk in the light.
May we be filled with joy
in following the way of Christ
so that others may come to know the truth.
Lord, hear us.

2. For unity in the church.
(pause)

Paul appeals for unity
among those who belong to Christ.
May we be tolerant in the church
of those whose views are different from our own
and acknowledge the struggles of all Christians
striving to be faithful to the gospel.
Lord, hear us.

3. For a sense of repentance.
(pause)

Jesus calls us to repent and believe the good news.
May we have courage to follow his teaching
bringing light to the world
and wholeness to its people.
Lord, hear us.

4. For an eagerness to follow the Lord's call.
(pause)

We are invited to follow the Lord,
and be part of God's plan to save all people.
May we be conscious of our responsibilities
to bear witness to the truth of the gospel
by the integrity of our lives.
Lord, hear us.

Priest/leader: God of the promises,
you bring us joy in following your way.
Listen to the prayers we make.
Through Christ our Lord. Amen.

Sunday 3

Year A

Sunday 4

Priest/ leader: 'Rejoice and be glad
for your reward will be great in heaven.'

God's powerful Word nourishes our spirit
and sustains us in our journey through life.
Strengthened by its teaching
we turn to the Lord for our needs.

1. For a desire to live by the truth.
(pause)

God commands us to live lives of integrity and humility,
understanding that God's way are not our ways.
May we live by the truth of the gospel,
obeying the commands of our God.
Lord, hear us.

2. For a desire to understand God's purposes.
(pause)

God's ways are often unknown to us
and God's purposes are sometimes hidden from us.
May we grow in trust of our God
knowing that in Christ
God has declared unimportant
what people regard as important in our world.
Lord, hear us.

3. For a desire to live as God wants.
(pause)

In the sermon on the mount,
Jesus teaches us what to value in life.
May our response be one of generous service
and a desire to understand
how we are to live as children of our God.
Lord, hear us.

4. For a desire to live by the beatitudes of Christ.
(pause)

May the teaching of Jesus
so fill our hearts
that the gospel values he preached and lived
may become part of the fabric of our lives
in what we do and what we consider important.
Lord, hear us.

Priest/ leader: God of all consolation,
your Son is the way to life.
Help us to follow his teaching
in how we live and in what we value.
We ask this through Christ our Lord. Amen.

Sunday 4

Sunday 5

Priest/ leader: 'You are the light of the world.'

God's Word has been broken for us
and we are nourished by its teaching.
Now we turn to our God
for what we need in the church
and in the community.

1. For a spirit of generosity.
(pause)

God commands us to share what we have
and to be generous to those in need.
May we be a people of God worthy of the name,
by our charity, our giving and our love.
Lord, hear us.

2. For a renewed faith in Christ crucified.
(pause)

Paul preached Christ crucified
and we too acknowledge the Christ
as central to our lives.
May the message of the cross
be in our hearts and minds
as we try to be faithful in following the Christ.
Lord, hear us.

3. For a desire to be the salt of the earth.
(pause)

May we be strengthened in our desire
to be the people of the gospel;
and may our faithfulness to its teaching
make our world and our communities
places of justice and truth.
Lord, hear us.

4. For a desire to be the light of the world.
(pause)

May our lives as Christians
so reflect the teaching of our Master
that all people will be attracted to the gospel
and come to know the truth about God
and about the Christ.
Lord, hear us.

Priest/ leader: God of all truth,
you command us to be salt and light in our world.
Help us to be faithful in following your Son.
We ask this through Christ our Lord. Amen.

Sunday 5

Year A

Sunday 6

Priest/ leader: 'I have not come to abolish the law but to fulfil it.'

God's Word has been broken
to nourish us with its teaching.
Strengthened by its message
we turn to our God for what we need.

1. For the gift of keeping the commandments.
(pause)

The commandments of God
bring life and fulfilment.
May we be strong in keeping them,
and may the Lord guide us
in the choices we make in life.
Lord, hear us.

2. For an awareness of God's purposes.
(pause)

The hidden purposes of God
are for our happiness and our wholeness.
May God's Spirit be at work in us
to teach us what is needed in our lives
and enable us to grow in God's love.
Lord, hear us.

3. For a desire to live by the gospel.
(pause)

The demands of the gospel are strong
and reach to every aspect of our lives.
May we be conscious of how we are to live,
reaching out to one another with forgiveness.
Lord, hear us.

4. For the gift of speaking the truth.
(pause)

May we be a people
devoted to the truth,
and may each of us strive
for that honesty, truthfulness and just living
that Jesus commanded of those who would follow him.
Lord, hear us.

Priest/ leader: God of all truth,
in you nothing is hidden.
Help us to be faithful followers of your Son.
For he is Lord, for ever and ever. Amen.

Sunday 6

Sunday 7

Priest/ leader: 'You must be perfect
as your heavenly Father is perfect.'

God's Word is broken for us
and calls us to lives of perfection.
Conscious of our littleness before God
we turn to the Lord
for what we need.

1. For a desire to keep God's commandments.
(pause)

God requires us to be holy
by keeping the commandments of the Lord.
May we strive to love one another
not bearing grudges but forgiving one another
as God commands.
Lord, hear us.

2. For a desire to belong to Christ.
(pause)

As temples of God

we are called to be worthy of the Spirit
that dwells within us.
May we be diligent in doing what God wants
even when it appears foolish by human standards
so that we may belong to Christ.
Lord, hear us.

3. For a true spirit of forgiveness.
(pause)

May we learn from the teaching of Jesus
to be generous in our forgiveness,
to acknowledge faults in ourselves and others
and to live in peace with one another
for the sake of the gospel.
Lord, hear us.

4. For a desire to love our enemies.
(pause)

The command of Jesus is that we love even our enemies.
By God's grace, may we be moved to forgive people
who have wronged us and,
especially in families,
may the love of Christ bring healing and forgiveness.
Lord, hear us.

Priest/ leader: God of love,
you command us to love one another
for your sake.
Help us live up to this high calling.
We ask this through Christ our Lord. Amen.

Sunday 7

Sunday 8

Priest/leader:
'Do not worry about tomorrow; tomorrow will take care of itself.'
The gospel encourages our trust in God's kindness.
Strengthened by its teaching, we approach our God
with our prayers and needs.

1. For renewed faith in God's love for each of us.
(pause)

God will not abandon us.
God will never forget us.
May the teaching of God's Word console us in time of trouble;
and may we grow in faith and love,
confident of God's care for each of us.
Lord, hear us.

2. For a desire to be good servants of the Lord.
(pause)

We are Christ's servants,
entrusted by him to live lives worthy of God's love.
May we be good servants of the Lord,
witnessing to the gospel by how we live
and what we value.
Lord, hear us.

3. For a right attitude towards possessions.
(pause)

May we take to heart the teaching of the gospel
avoiding excess in how we live;
and by attitudes towards what we eat and what we wear
may we deepen our faith in our God
who cares for all the creatures of the world.
Lord, hear us.

4. For a desire to serve God only.
(pause)

We cannot be slaves to two masters.
May the teaching of Christ so move us
that we will determine to serve God rather than money,
setting our hearts on what is required
for the coming of God's kingdom.
Lord, hear us.

Priest/leader:
God of all consolation,
may your kingdom come!
Listen to the prayers we make; and grant them.
Through Christ our Lord. Amen.

Sunday 8

Sunday 9

Priest/leader:
'The one who does the will of my Father
will enter the kingdom of heaven.'
God's Word has been broken for us
and its teaching nourishes us for life's journey.
Strengthened by its message,
we turn to our God for what we need.

1. For a desire to live as God wants.
(pause)

May we be filled with a desire to do God's will
and to live according to the gospel,
that, holding fast to the teaching of the Lord,
we may be worthy of the blessings
promised by our God.
Lord, hear us.

2. For a deeper faith in God.
(pause)

Faith makes us right with God.
May our faith in Christ grow each day
and may we witness to what we believe
by lives that reflect the teaching of the gospel
and the commandments of the Lord.
Lord, hear us.

3. For a determination to work for God's kingdom.
(pause)

God's kingdom is promised to those who do God's will.
May our lives in the church and in the community
be founded on a desire to live God's way
striving for justice in society
and caring for those in need.
Lord, hear us.

4. For an eagerness to listen to God's Word.
(pause)

May we be open to God's Word and God's teaching
in the Scripture and in the community;
and, like a house built on a rock,
may we be constant in our faith journey
with our God.
Lord, hear us.

Priest/leader:
God of all creation,
we thank you for your gift of faith.
Strengthen us in our journey
and grant what we need.
Through Christ our Lord. Amen.

Sunday 9

Sunday 10

Priest/leader:
'What I want is mercy not sacrifice.'

God's powerful Word is food for our journey in faith.
Nourished by its teaching, we turn to our God
for what we need.

1. For a desire to know God's will.
(pause)

May we be constant in seeking God's will
for the church and for the community.
And may our love and service
be deep and lasting
until the Lord comes.
Lord, hear us.

2. For the gifts of faith and love.
(pause)

Like Abraham, our father in faith,
may we be filled with the gift of hope,
believing the promises of God
who raised Jesus to life,
reconciling us to our God and our world.
Lord, hear us.

3. For a desire to follow Christ.
(pause)

Like Matthew, may we follow the Christ,
alert to his call and eager to be his disciples
by how we live and what we consider important in life.
Lord, hear us.

4. For a right attitude towards religion.
(pause)

May we not be contented only by the rituals of our faith
but may we seek to reflect our relationship with our God
through our actions towards others,
especially those in need,
Lord, hear us.

Priest/Leader:
God of our ancestors, you demand mercy rather than ritual.
Strengthen our resolve to live by your way
and grant what we need,
Through Christ our Lord. Amen.

Sunday 10

Sunday 11

Priest/leader:
'I have carried you on eagle's wings.'
Our God is a God who cares for us and loves us.
Strengthened by God's Word
we turn to the Lord
for what we need.

1. For a sense of belonging to God.
(pause)
God has declared us a kingdom of priests,
a nation consecrated to the Lord.
May our sense of belonging to God
be reflected in lives of faithfulness
to God's teaching.
Lord, hear us.

2. For joyful trust in our God.
(pause)
Christ has died for us
and reconciled us to our God.
May we be filled with joyful trust
in God's goodness
and live always as a people of hope.
Lord, hear us.

3. For a sense of mission in the world.
(pause)
We are commanded to bring healing
to our world.
May we be a people of joy and hope,
bringing peace, forgiveness
and a sense of purpose
to our restless world.
Lord, hear us.

4. For a sense of renewed faith
in God's purposes.
(pause)
May we be true followers of the Christ,
proclaiming God's kingdom in our world
by acts of kindness and acceptance and love.
And may people everywhere learn
of God's purposes
by our faithfulness to gospel teaching.
Lord, hear us.

Priest/leader:
God of the promises,
we believe in your love and care for all.
Grant what we need
to proclaim your kingdom
for you are Lord,
for ever and ever. Amen.

Sunday 11

- 47 -

Year A

Sunday 12

Priest/leader: 'Do not be afraid.'
The good news of God's Word
has been broken for us,
and we are commanded to approach our God
with love and confidence.
We now reflect on what we need
as God's people in God's world.

1. For confidence in God's love.
(pause)

Jeremiah, the prophet of God,
committed his cause to the Lord,
confident of God's goodness and care.
May we too learn to trust our God
and turn to the Lord in times of trouble.
Lord, hear us.

2. For an awareness of what God has done for us.
(pause)

Through Adam's fault,
the power of sin entered the world
and threatened to destroy our race.
May we be conscious
of what God has done in Christ
breaking the bonds of sin in our lives
and enabling us to live as God's children.
Lord, hear us.

3. For the strength to overcome fear.
(pause)

When we are afraid for our world,
our families and ourselves,
may we be comforted by the teaching
that God is ruler of all the world
and Lord of all that is and is to come.
Lord, hear us.

4. For courage to proclaim the truth.
(pause)

We are commanded to proclaim the truth
about God and about the Christ.
By the integrity of our lives
and the values we profess
may we be authentic witnesses
to the way of Christ.
Lord, hear us.

Sunday 12

Priest/leader:
God of all consolation,
you free us from fear
and give us confidence in life.
Grant what we need
though Christ our Lord. Amen.

Sunday 13

Priest /leader: 'You are alive for God in Christ Jesus.'

The good news of God's Word
fills us with hope
as we recall what God has done for us.
In a spirit of confidence, we turn to the Lord
for what we need.

1. For the gift of hospitality.
(pause)

May we be hospitable in our lives,
caring for those who are in need
and may we be generous
towards those in our society
without love and without hope.
Lord, hear us.

2. For a desire to share what we have.
(pause)

May we be moved by the teaching
of the gospel
to consider our attitude to what we own
and may we learn to share our abundance
with those who have less in our world.
Lord, hear us.

3. For a desire to live a new life in Christ.
(pause)

When we were baptised
we were raised to new life in Christ.
May we be constant in overcoming
the power of sin in our lives
and by our faithfulness to the gospel
show that we live for Christ
and not for sin.
Lord, hear us.

4. For the grace to make right decisions in life.
(pause)

May we be guided by the teaching of Jesus
in making important decisions in life
so that what we basically value in life
may be in accordance with what God wants.
Lord, hear us.

Priest /leader: Generous God,
you sent your son to die for us.
May we too be generous in your service
and in caring for others.
We ask this through Christ our Lord. Amen.

Sunday 13

Year A

Sunday 14

Priest /leader:' My yoke is easy and my burden light.'
God's Word challenges yet comforts us.
Nourished by its teaching,
we turn to the Lord
for what we need
in our church and in our world.

1. For a spirit of joy.
(pause)

The Lord commands us to rejoice
because God is ruler of all the earth.
May our faith in God's goodness
grow stronger each day
and may we experience joy
in the presence of our God.
Lord, hear us.

2. For a desire to be possessed
by God's Spirit.
(pause)

May we be faithful to our Baptism promises
and so desire to live God's way
that the Holy Spirit may possess our lives
and guide us in what we do.
Lord, hear us.

3. For a spirit of humility before God.
(pause)

May we be humble towards the Lord
aware of God's power in heaven and on earth
and may we be conscious of our littleness
in God's presence
and the immensity of God's mysterious love.
Lord, hear us.

4. For an awareness of God's kindness.
(pause)

May we be strong in faith
and in living the gospel
acknowledging that the kindness of our God
makes the yoke easy and the burden light.
Lord, hear us.

Priest /leader: God of all kindness,
you bless your people in life and in death.
Make us eager to live your way
and to proclaim your truth
in all that we do.
We ask this through Christ our Lord. Amen.

Sunday 14

Sunday 15

Priest /leader: 'Listen, anyone who has ears!'
God's word has been broken for us
and we have listened to its teaching.
Now we reflect on its meaning for us
turning the Lord for what we need.

1. For a deeper understanding of God's Word.
(pause)

May we grow in understanding
the Word of God in the Bible,
learning to apply its teaching
in the church and in the world,
as it carries out God will.
Lord, hear us.

2. For a deeper appreciation of God's creation.
(pause)

All creation is a witness of God's purposes.
May we always respect our universe
and from its beauty, integrity and nature
deepen our understanding
of what God wants of us
and how we should treat our world.
Lord, hear us.

3. For a desire to live the way of Christ.
(pause)

May we be guided by the teaching of Jesus
in all that we value
and hold dearest,
and by our living the gospel
may others be drawn to the truth of God.
Lord, hear us.

4. For the coming of the kingdom of God.
(pause)

The teaching of Jesus reveals to us
God's purposes for the coming of the kingdom.
May we be faithful followers of the Christ
listening to that teaching
and bearing fruit by our obedience
to God's Word.
Lord, hear us.

Priest /leader: God of the promises,
may your kingdom come!
Help us to be faithful to your Word
producing a rich harvest
in the church and in the world.
We ask this through Christ our Lord. Amen.

Sunday 15

Year A

Sunday 16

Priest /leader:
'The Spirit helps us in our weakness.'
Nourished by God's Word
and comforted by God's Spirit,
we turn in prayer to our God
for the needs of the church
and the world.

1. For a sense of God's majesty.
(pause)

May we be humble in the Lord's presence,
aware of God's power and might,
yet thankful for the mildness of God
and the gentleness of the Lord
towards the creation God has made.
Lord, hear us.

2. For compassion towards others.
(pause)

God commands us to be kind
towards one another.
May we be faithful to that teaching
by our compassion, our tolerance
and our forgiveness;
and may we be aware of our own need
for repentance for the times we do wrong.
Lord, hear us.

3. For an openness to God's Spirit.
(pause)

May we welcome the Spirit of God
into our lives
and may we be open to that Spirit
when we are confused or anxious
about what to say and how to pray.
Lord, hear us.

4. For a desire for the coming of God's kingdom.
(pause)

May we be eager for the coming
 of God's kingdom
and by lives that reflect gospel values
may God be glorified
and the good news spread
in our community and in our world.
Lord, hear us.

Sunday 16

Priest /leader: God of the universe,
may your kingdom come!
Help us to do your will
and to be faithful to your teaching.
We ask this through Christ our Lord. Amen.

Sunday 17

Priest/leader:
'I will give you a heart wise and shrewd', says the Lord.
God's Word has been broken for us
and God's wisdom has filled our minds.
With confidence we turn to the Lord
for what we need.

1. For the gift of wisdom.
(pause)

May we be people of discernment,
learning to judge what is right in God's sight
and may we be reluctant to criticise others
by word or attitude.
Lord, hear us.

2. For a desire to imitate Christ.
(pause)

Jesus is our brother,
the head of the community called the church.
May we imitate him as our eldest brother
and by our generosity and love
share the glory promised by God.
Lord, hear us.

3. For enthusiasm in following the way of Christ.
(pause)

May we be moved by the teaching of Jesus
to be enthusiastic and generous
in seeking the kingdom,
eager for its coming in our church
and in our world.
Lord, hear us.

4. For tolerance in the church.
(pause)

May we acknowledge Jesus
as Lord and Head of the church
who values both old and new in the church;
and may be tolerant of one another
as we strive to discover God's will
for the church and the world.
Lord, hear us.

Priest /leader:
God of the universe,
may your kingdom come!
Teach us your ways.
Fill us with your wisdom
and help us to love one another.
We ask this through Christ our Lord. Amen.

Sunday 18

Priest /leader: 'Nothing can come between us
and the love of Christ.'
This is the good news
that we have heard.
God's Word has nourished us
and we turn to our God for what we need.

1. For confidence in God's goodness.
(pause)

We are taught to be discerning
about what is important in life.
May we never lose sight
of God's goodness and love
and of the promises made
to the church and all peoples.
Lord, hear us.

2. For a renewed sense of unity with Christ.
(pause)

Paul teaches us
that nothing can separate us from Christ.
May this teaching
renew our sense of unity with Christ
and with each other;
and may it sustain us in time of suffering,
distress and loss.
Lord, hear us.

3. For a deeper awareness of God's love for us.
(pause)

God's love is so great
that nothing can overcome it.
May we deepen our understanding
of God's mysterious love
and give thanks for it
by lives of faithfulness to the way of Christ.
Lord, hear us.

4. For generosity towards others.
(pause)

Jesus fed the five thousand
from the few resources he had.
May we learn to imitate the Master
sharing the little we have,
knowing that what is little
can become abundant in God's sight.
Lord, hear us.

Priest /leader: God of all goodness,
you are bountiful to all your people.
Help us to be your faithful followers
in the church and in the community.
We ask this through Christ our Lord. Amen.

Sunday 18

Sunday 19

Priest /leader:
'Truly you are the son of God.'
God's Word has been broken for us
and we are comforted by its teaching.
We recall the needs of our church
and our world
and present them to the Lord.

1. For an appreciation of God's gentleness and love.
(pause)

God is revealed to Isaiah
not in storms or earthquake
but in the gentle breeze.
May we grow in respect and love
towards our God who is revealed
in gentleness and tenderness.
Lord, hear us.

2. For the Jewish people.
(pause)

Paul prayed for the Jewish people
and we too commend them
to our loving God.
May they be faithful to the ancient covenant
and remain steadfast in their search for the truth.
Lord, hear us.

3. For a deepening of our life of prayer.
(pause)

Jesus went off into the hills to pray.
May we relish the time spent in prayer
and may these times of reflection and peace
give us renewed strength
on our journey with God.
Lord, hear us.

4. For courage to follow Christ.
(pause)

Like Peter, may we have the courage
to follow Christ
and may our faith in Christ sustain us
especially in times of great stress
and personal misfortune.
Lord, hear us.

Priest /leader:
God of storm and earthquake,
you are mighty and powerful
yet you reveal yourself
to the little ones of the earth.
Hear the prayers we make to you
through Christ our Lord. Amen.

Year A

Sunday 20

Priest/leader: 'Son of David, take pity on us!'
Nourished by God's Word,
we approach the Lord in a spirit of humility
seeking what we need
for our church and our world.

1. For an openness to people of other faiths.
(pause)
We believe in our God who is Ruler of all the earth,
who cares for all the people of the world.
May we too respect people of other faiths
who search for truth and meaning
in their journey through life.
Lord, hear us.

2. For the Jewish people.
(pause)
We acknowledge that the Jewish people
were the first to receive God's good news.
May we be conscious of their special place
in God's plan of salvation
and be vigilant in promoting harmony
among people of different traditions and cultures.
Lord, hear us.

3. For perseverance in prayer.
(pause)
May we be confident in prayer
imitating those who pleaded with the Lord
and may we be open to what God wants in our lives
as the basis for all our prayer.
Lord, hear us.

4. For the grace to be faithful witnesses.
(pause)

May the community that is called the church
be a faithful witness to its Lord
and by its faithfulness to the example of Jesus
may people everywhere be brought to faith.
Lord, hear us.

Priest/leader: God of the promises,
you surprise us with the answers to our prayers.
Help us to be good servants of your Son.
We ask this through Christ our Lord. Amen.

Sunday 20

Sunday 21

Priest/leader:
'You are the Christ, the Son of living God.'
God's Word has been broken for us
and nourishes us in our faith journey.
We now recall the needs of our church
and our communities
as we turn to the Lord in prayer.

1. For leaders in the churches.
(pause)

We pray for those who exercise leadership
in the churches.
May they be people of faith and wisdom;
and by their preaching of the gospel
may people everywhere
acknowledge Jesus as the Christ of God.
Lord, hear us.

2. For a deeper awareness of God's majesty and goodness.
(pause)

With Paul, may we be filled with wonder
at the majesty of God.
May we always reverence our God,
acknowledging the Lord as a living God
whose nature and purpose are beyond
our words and imagination.
Lord, hear us.

3. For preachers and teachers in the churches.
(pause)

We pray for those who preach and teach in our churches.
May they be constant in pointing us to the Christ of God
and may we support them
and encourage them in their ministry.
Lord, hear us.

4. For a deepening of faith in all who believe.
(pause)

May all of us be renewed in faith this day
and like Peter who confessed Jesus as God's Son
renew our commitment to follow the way of Christ
by lives that take seriously the teaching of the gospel.
Lord, hear us.

Priest/leader: Living God and Father,
you have revealed yourself to us
in Jesus your Son.
Help us follow his way and his teaching
for he is Lord, for ever and ever. Amen.

Sunday 21

Sunday 22

Priest/leader: 'Take up your cross and follow me.'
God's Word nourishes us,
giving us the strength and the courage
to live as God wants.
Refreshed by its teaching,
we approach our God
for what we need.

1. For the gift to persevere in God's service.
(pause)

The call of God is a call to sacrifice.
May we be faithful in following God's way
in the face of temptation and insult,
and may we support one another
in the church and in the community
by the values we own and the truth we profess.
Lord, hear us.

2. For a desire to discover God's will.
(pause)

May we always seek to find God's will
in the church and in the community
and may we have the courage to stand up for what we believe
even when that is unpopular with others,
Lord, hear us.

3. For an acceptance of the cross of Christ.
(pause)

May we acknowledge the mysterious will of God
especially in times of trouble;
and may we be generous towards others,
carrying the crosses that life brings,
comforting and supporting one another
in our journey through life.
Lord, hear us.

4. For a desire to understand what is important in life.
(pause)

May we understand that God's ways are not our ways;
and may we be concerned about what is of lasting value
so that God's plan for each of us may be fulfilled,
bringing us happiness in doing what God wants.
Lord, hear us.

Priest/leader:
Loving God,
you provide for us always.
Deepen our confidence in your love for us
and grant what we need.
Through Christ our Lord. Amen.

Sunday 22

Sunday 23

Priest/leader: 'Where two or three meet in my name,
I shall be with them.'
We meet in the name of Christ
and we have listened to God's Word
broken for us.
With renewed confidence, we turn to our God
for what we need.

1. For the courage to witness to our faith.
(pause)

May we have courage to stand up for what we believe,
correcting those who oppose the truth,
by lives that witness to the gospel
and values that reflect the way of Christ.
Lord, hear us.

2. For a desire to love one another.
(pause)

Paul sums up the commandments of God
by his teaching that we must love one another.
May we strive to carry out the command of love
by lives that are faithful to the teaching of the Lord.
Lord, hear us.

3. For peace in our families and communities.
(pause)

May the Lord's teaching compel us to forgive one another
especially in family quarrels;
and may our desire to forgive one another
overcome the hurts we may have experienced.
Lord, hear us.

4. For an awareness of Christ's presence among us.
(pause)

May we acknowledge Christ's presence among us
in the church and in the community;
and may his presence be a source of strength for us
in our prayers and in all of our lives.
Lord, hear us.

Priest/leader:
God of all consolation
your Son is with us always.
May we be encouraged by his presence
and renewed in our confidence of your love.
We ask this through Christ our Lord. Amen.

Sunday 23

Sunday 24

Priest/leader: 'The Lord is compassion and love.'
God's Word has been broken for us
and its teaching nourishes our spirit.
Strengthened by that teaching,
we approach our God for what we need.

1. For the gift of gentleness.
(pause)

God commands us to avoid anger and resentment.
May we have the gift of gentleness towards others,
not returning evil for evil
but striving for that compassion and love
that we hope for from the Lord.
Lord, hear us.

2. For a sense of Christ's presence among us.
(pause)

May we be moved by a sense of Christ's presence;
and by lives that reflect his teaching
show forth the love and compassion of Christ
who is Lord of both living and dead.
Lord, hear us.

3. For a desire to forgive.
(pause)

Jesus commands us to forgive one another.
May we take his teaching with such seriousness
that we may be known as people of forgiveness,
eager to overlook the hurt people do to us.
Lord, hear us.

4. For a sense of God's generous love.
(pause)

The Gospel teaches us that God's love is boundless.
May we grow in understanding God's love
so that we may be gentle with ourselves
and with others.
Lord, hear us**.**

Priest/leader:
God of compassion,
fill us with a sense of your love for us
and grant what we need.
Through Christ our Lord. Amen.

Sunday 25

Priest/leader:
'The last will be first and the first last.'
We have heard God's Word
and been strengthened by its teaching.
How we turn to our loving God
for what we need
in the church and in the country.

1. For a sense of God's majesty.
(pause)

My thoughts are not your thoughts, says the Lord
and my ways are not your ways.
May we be comforted by a sense of God's majesty,
open to whatever God has planned for us in the world.
Lord, hear us.

2. For a desire to be pleasing to God.
(pause)

May we be anxious to please our God
by lives that reflect sound teaching
and by avoiding anything in life
that is unworthy of the gospel of Christ.
Lord, hear us.

3. For a deeper understanding of God's gracious love.
(pause)

May the love of God increase in our hearts
and may we be constantly comforted
by the immensity of God's love
who cares for even the least important in creation.
Lord, hear us.

4. For an awareness of the compassion of our God.
(pause)

God does not judge by human standards
and God's generous love is beyond our understanding.
May we learn to trust in the compassion of our God
who turns the world's values upside down;
and may we be generous towards one another
as God is generous towards us.
Lord, hear us.

Priest/leader:
God of all mercies,
listen to our prayers for what we need.
For you are Lord, forever and ever. Amen.

Sunday 25

Sunday 26

Priest/leader:
'Jesus Christ is Lord,
to the glory of God the Father.'
We have been strengthened and nourished
by God's Word, broken for us.
Encouraged by its teaching,
we turn to our God for our needs.

1. For a spirit of generosity.
(pause)

Our God is compassion and love,
eager to forgive when we repent of sin.
May we too be a people of forgiveness,
not holding grudges but accepting people
when they turn to us in need.
Lord, hear us.

2. For an understanding
of the majesty of Christ.
(pause)

Christ emptied himself for us
and became a slave for our sake.
May we grow to understand the heights
to which God has raised him
and worship him as Lord of all.
Lord, hear us.

3. For a desire to live by the truth.
(pause)

May our yes be yes and our no be no;
and may we be people of the truth
faithful in what we promise,
especially in living the gospel.
Lord, hear us.

4. For a desire to spread God's kingdom.
(pause)

God's kingdom is mysteriously present
among us
and no one is excluded
who tries to be faithful to God's way.
May we not judge who is fit for the kingdom
but rely on God's mercy on us
and on all who are children of God.

Priest/leader:
God of mercy,
have pity on all your children.
Teach us to forgive others as you forgive us.
We ask this through Christ our Lord. Amen.

Sunday 27

Priest/leader:
'The stone rejected by the builder became the keystone.'
God's broken Word is powerful and disturbing
Strengthened by its teaching,
we approach our God for what we need.

1. For the gift of gratitude to God.
(pause)

May we be a people of thankfulness -
aware of what God has done for us
in history and in our lives today;
and may our gratitude to God
be reflected in our lives of concern
for other people.
Lord, hear us.

2. For the gift of peace.
(pause)

May we experience peace in our lives -
the peace that comes from listening to the gospel,
reflecting on its meaning
and living by its teaching.
Lord, hear us.

3. For the gift of producing good fruit.
(pause)

May our lives be fruitful in God's service.
and, by our living of the gospel teaching,
may God's kingdom come;
and may we share with others
the gifts that God has generously given us.
Lord, hear us.

4. For the gift of wisdom.
(pause)

The stone rejected by the builder
became the key stone.
May we have the gift of wisdom,
able to read the signs of the times
and open to what God wants
in the church and in the community
Lord, hear us.

Priest/leader:
God of all consolation,
your truth sets us free,
your way leads to life.
Grant what we need through Christ our Lord. Amen

Sunday 27

Sunday 28

Priest/leader:
'The Lord will wipe away our tears'
The Word of God consoles and comforts us.
Strengtheened by its teaching,
we ask our God for what we need.

1. For a deeper understanding of God's love.
(pause)

God's love is for all people
and God invites all people to the kingdom.
May we not be narrow in our understanding
of God's love.
but, like our God, be accepting of all people
as God has accepted us.
Lord, hear us.

2. For a desire to do what God wants.
(pause)

Like Paul, we have experienced good times
and bad,
times of poverty and times of plenty.
Like him, may we bless God always,
eager only to do what God wants,
depending on God's lavish concern for us all.
Lord, hear us.

3. For a openness to what God wants.
(pause)

May we open to what God wants
and reach out to others in love
so that God's kingdom might be proclaimed
and people come to understand God's love
for all the people of the world.
Lord, hear us.

4. For a deepening of faith.
(pause)

May we grow in faith each day,
constantly reviewing what we value in life,
and witnessing to the teaching of our Master
by lives of integrity, honesty and truth.
Lord, hear us.

Priest/leader:
God of our ancestors,
may your kingdom come!
Keep us faithful to your ways
and grant what we need.
Through Christ our Lord. Amen.

Sunday 28

Sunday 29

Priest/leader:
'Give to God what belongs to God.'
The Word of God
nourishes us in our journey through life.
We have listened to its teaching
and now turn to our God for what we need.

1. For an awareness that God is Lord of all.
(pause)

God is the ruler of all the world -
past, present and to come.
May we be comforted by this teaching
and submit ourselves to the care of the one
who is Lord of all.
Lord, hear us.

2. For faith in action.
(pause)

Paul commended the Christian churches
for their faith in action.
May we too be the people of God
who take seriously the way of Christ
in how we live and what we value.
Lord, hear us.

3. For a right attitude towards God.
(pause)

May we honour our God in all of life
by what we say and what we do;
and may we be witnesses to the teaching
we have received
in what we consider of lasting value in life.
Lord, hear us.

4. For the gift of honesty.
(pause)

May we be people of the truth,
and honest in all that we do;
and may we stand up for what we believe
in the church and in the community.
Lord, hear us.

Priest/leader:
Lord God of the Universe
we worship you and thank you
for the gifts you give us.
Grant what we need.
Through Christ our Lord. Amen.

Sunday 29

Year A

Sunday 30

Priest/leader:
'You must love your neighbour as yourself.'
God's powerful Word
nourishes us in life's journey.
We have listened to its teaching
and now turn to our God
for what we need.

1. For the gift of compassion.
(pause)

Like the children of Israel,
we are commanded by our God
to love one another.
May we have the gift of compassion
for one another in the church and the community.
Lord, hear us.

2. For the gift of deep faith in God.
(pause)

Paul commends the churches
for the example they provide
because of their faith in God.
May we too deepen our faith in our God
becoming servants in God's world.
Lord, hear us.

3. For the gift of love.
(pause)

The greatest commandment is to love God
and to love our neighbour.
May we be known as a community of love
and acknowledged every day
as a people who care for one another.
Lord, hear us.

4. For the gift of service.
(pause)

We are commended to love
our neighbour as ourselves.
May we be generous in the service
of God and of one another,
especially toward those who need our care,
our compassion and our charity.
Lord, hear us.

Priest/leader:
Generous God,
you give us all we need
in the church and in the community.
Help us be your true servants.
We ask you this through Christ our Lord.
Amen.

Sunday 30

Sunday 31

Priest/leader:
'The greatest among you
must be your servant.'
God's Word has been broken for us
and we are nourished by its teaching.
Strengthened by that Word
we turn to our God for what we need.

1. For leaders in the churches.
(pause)

May all who exercise leadership
in the churches
be people of integrity and justice.
May they be faithful in preaching
God's good news
and honest in practising what they preach.
Lord, hear us.

2. For a desire to spread the good news.
(pause)

May we be eager to pass on the good news
about God's love and God's Word,
not simply by what we teach
but by what we value and how we live.
Lord, hear us.

3. For a spirit of compassion.
(pause)

May the good news by which we live
move us to compassion for others
so that our way of life does not burden others
but frees them to live as children of God.
Lord, hear us.

4. For a spirit of humility.
(pause)

May we understand our worth in God's sight
and rejoice that we are God's children.
And in the imitation of Christ
may we live for others,
following his teaching to be servants
in the community.
Lord, hear us.

Priest/leader:
God of consolation,
you sent your son, Jesus,
to be servant of all.
Teach us to imitate him
and to care for one another.
We ask this through Christ our Lord. Amen.

Sunday 31

Sunday 32

Priest/leader:
'You do not know the day or the hour.'

God's Word challenges us to stay awake.
Strengthened by its teaching,
we turn with confidence to our God
for what we need.

1. For the gift of wisdom.
(pause)
God's Wisdom is God's plan for all people.
May we too seek the Wisdom of God
so that we know what is of lasting value in life
and lead lives that accord with God's will.
Lord, hear us.

2. For trust in God's goodness.
(pause)
We commend to our God
those who have fallen asleep in the Lord.
We confess our faith in God's power to save
confident that our God will care for us
in the life to come.
Lord, hear us.

3. For the grace to be ready when the Lord comes.
(pause)
When the Lord visits us,
may we be ready to greet him.
When the needs of our neighbours are known to us,
may we respond with love,
recognising the Lord's presence
in those who are suffering in our world.
Lord, hear us.

4. For a serious desire to follow Christ.
(pause)
May we be alert at all times,
taking seriously the teaching of the Lord
by lives that live out gospel values
and actions that proclaim the way of Christ.
Lord, hear us.

Priest/leader: God of the promises,
you never leave your people.
Comfort and strengthen us in times of trouble
and grant what we need.
Through Christ our Lord.
Amen.

Sunday 33

Priest/leader:
'Well done, good and faithful servant.'
God's Word, broken for us,
comforts and encourages us in life's journey.
Strengthened by its teaching,
we turn to our God
for what we need.

1. For generosity of spirit.
(pause)

May we be generous in God's service,
alert to the needs of others in the community
and eager to share with them
the gifts we have received from God.
Lord, hear us.

2. For an openness to God in our lives.
(pause)

May we be alert to God's presence in our lives
and like children of the light
look for ways to be of service to others
when we see them in need.
Lord, hear us.

3. For a desire to be God's faithful people.
(pause)

We acknowledge that God has called us
to lives of faithful service.
May we strive always to use God's gifts wisely
in the church and in the community.
Lord, hear us.

4. For a right attitude in our approach to God.
(pause)

May our approach to God be one of love
rather than fear
and in serving God and our neighbour
may God's love spur us on
helping us do what is right in God's sight.
Lord, hear us.

Priest/leader: God of all consolation,
your reveal yourself to us as a God of love.
Help us respond to you in love
and grant what we need.
Through Christ our Lord. Amen.

Sunday 34 Christ the King

Priest/leader:
'He must be king until he has put all things under his feet.'
The Word of God comforts and strengthens us.
On this feast of Christ the King,
we have been nourished by its teaching
and we turn to our God with confidence
for all our needs.

1. For a deeper faith in God's love for us.
(pause)

God is our shepherd
with a concern for even the weakest of the flock.
May we deepen our faith in God's love for us
and rejoice that our God cares for each one of us.
Lord, hear us.

2. For a deeper faith in God's power to save us.
(pause)

Christ has been raised from the dead,
the first fruits of those who have fallen asleep.
May we grow in faith
in God's power to save us from sin and death
and rejoice always in the Lordship
of Christ our King.
Lord, hear us.

3. For a desire to serve Christ our King.
(pause)

May we be faithful servants of our king
living lives that reflect the values of his kingdom
and caring for those in need in the church
and in the community.
Lord, hear us.

4. For a desire to be a kingdom people.
(pause)

Christ the King is our ruler -
he proclaims justice, love and peace.
May these be the marks of God's people;
and may we desire to live by the gospel
so that God's kingdom may come in our world.
Lord, hear us.

Priest/leader: Almighty God, Ruler of the Universe,
we worship you and honour your name.
Grant what we need to be faithful servants
in the kingdom of Christ
for he is Lord, for ever and ever. Amen.

Sunday 34